P9-APQ-734

CLIMATE CHANGE
iN THE ANTARCTIC

STUART BAKER

Marshall Cavendish
Benchmark

New York

This edition first published in 2010 in the United States of America
by Marshall Cavendish Benchmark.

Marshall Cavendish Benchmark
99 White Plains Road
Tarrytown, NY 10591
www.marshallcavendish.us

First published in 2009 by
MACMILLAN EDUCATION AUSTRALIA PTY LTD
15–19 Claremont Street, South Yarra 3141

Visit our website at www.macmillan.com.au or go directly to www.macmillanlibrary.com.au

Associated companies and representatives throughout the world.

Library of Congress Cataloging-in-Publication Data

Baker, Stuart.
  In the Antarctic / by Stuart Baker.
    p. cm. – (Climate change)
  Includes index.
  ISBN 978-0-7614-4438-1
  1. Antarctica–Juvenile literature. I. Title.
  G863.B37 2010
  508.3398'9–dc22

                              2009005766

Edited by Sally Woollett
Text and cover design by Christine Deering
Page layout by Christine Deering
Illustrations by Richard Morden
Photo research by Legend Images

Printed in the United States

Acknowledgments
The author and the publisher are grateful to the following for permission to reproduce
copyright material:

Front cover photograph: Adélie penguins on melting ice floe, Ross Sea, Antarctica, courtesy
of Tui De Roy/Minden Pictures/Getty Images
Photos courtesy of:
Image by Jan Lieser, Antarctic Climate & Ecosystems Cooperative Research Centre, with
helicopter courtesy www.3Dkitbuilder.com and TheyerGFX Pty Ltd, **25**; Australian Antarctic
Division © Commonwealth of Australia Photograph by Mathew Godbold, **15**; Australian
Antarctic Division © Commonwealth of Australia Photograph by Peter Mcgill, **29** (top);
Doug Allan/Getty Images, **11**; Suzi Eszterhas/Getty Images, **16**; George F. Mobley/National
Geographic/Getty Images, **9**; Maria Stenzel/Getty Images, **20**; Norbert Wu/Getty Images, **12**;
International Polar Foundation/Johan Berte, **27**; © steve estvanik/iStockphoto, **22, 29** (bottom);
NASA, **19**; NASA/Goddard Space Flight Center Scientific Visualization Studio, **8, 13** (top and
bottom); Emily Stone, National Science Foundation, **24, 30**; Photolibrary/Index Stock, **17**;
Photolibrary/Bernhard Edmaier/Science Photo Library, **14**; Wikimedia Commons, photo by
Hannes Grobe 15:50, 13 January 2007 (UTC), Alfred Wegener Institute for Polar- and Marine
Research, Bremerhaven, **10**

While every care has been taken to trace and acknowledge copyright, the publisher tenders
their apologies for any accidental infringement where copyright has proved untraceable.
Where the attempt has been unsuccessful, the publisher welcomes information that would
redress the situation.

1 3 5 6 4 2

Contents

| Glossary Words | When a word is printed in **bold**, you can look up its meaning in the Glossary on page 31. |

Climate Change

Earth has been warming and cooling for millions of years. During the **Ice Age**, large areas of Europe and Canada were covered with **glaciers**. Earth's climate was 5.4–9°Fahrenheit (3–5°Celsius) cooler than it is today. The most recent Ice Age ended 20,000 years ago.

Fact ZONE

Today, Earth's average surface temperature is 59°F (15°C).

Rising Temperatures

Temperatures across the world are rising at a rate faster than ever before. Earth's average temperature has risen by 1.08°F (0.6°C) in the past one hundred years. The ten hottest years on record occurred over the past fourteen years. The hottest year ever recorded was 2005. This **global warming** may be enough to cause changes in weather patterns, which is commonly referred to as **climate change**.

Earth's Climate Zones

Earth can be divided into four main types of climate zones:

- Arctic
- Temperate
- Tropical
- Antarctic

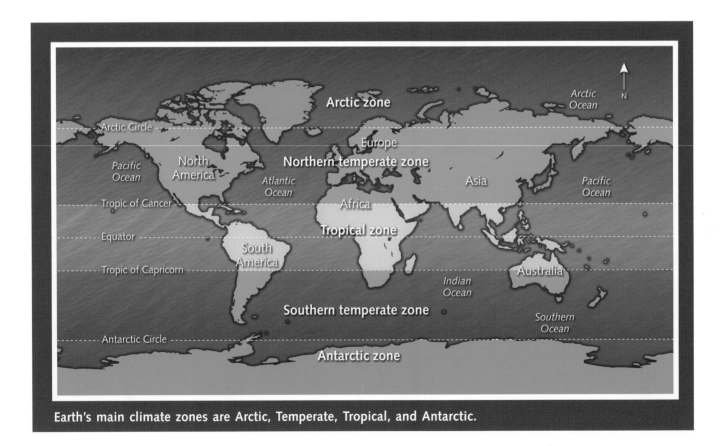

Earth's main climate zones are Arctic, Temperate, Tropical, and Antarctic.

The Antarctic Region

Antarctica is the southernmost continent in the world and surrounds the South Pole. The Antarctic region consists of the frozen continent, the Southern Ocean, and the isolated sub-Antarctic islands.

Ice and Snow

The Antarctic is one of the harshest environments on Earth. It is a cold desert mostly buried under ice and snow. Antarctica is covered by a thick **ice sheet** and thousands of **glaciers**, and the surrounding ocean contains a floating **ice shelf** and **icebergs**. In the winter **sea ice** forms as the surrounding ocean freezes. This increases the size of the continent by 50 percent.

No one lives permanently in the Antarctic, but a number of scientific research bases have been established there.

Fact ZONE

Antarctica is the windiest continent on Earth, with speeds of up to 186 miles (300 kilometers) per hour recorded.

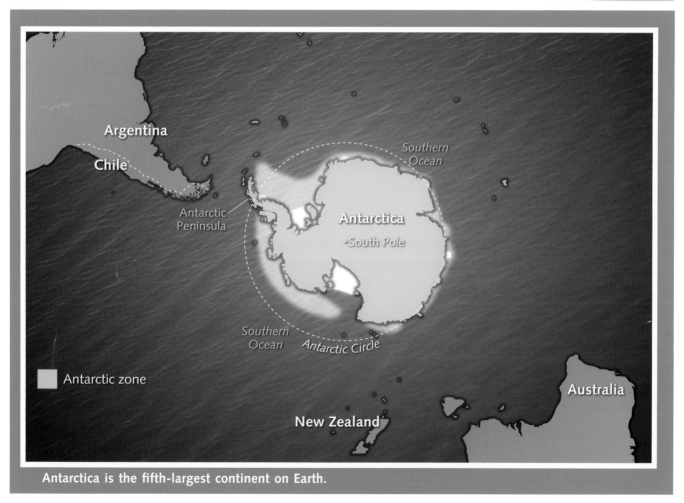

Argentina
Chile
Southern Ocean
Antarctic Peninsula
Antarctica
South Pole
Southern Ocean
Antarctic Circle
Antarctic zone
Australia
New Zealand

Antarctica is the fifth-largest continent on Earth.

Global Warming and Greenhouse Gases

Global warming is caused by the **greenhouse effect**. **Greenhouse gases** trap the heat from the sun in Earth's **atmosphere**. This heat leads to an increase in Earth's surface temperature.

Greenhouse Gases

Greenhouse gases occur naturally in Earth's atmosphere, but human activities contribute to these gases. These human activities are increasing as the world's population increases.

Scientists now agree that in recent decades the amount of greenhouse gases in the atmosphere has increased. More of the sun's heat is being trapped, leading to further global warming. The term "global warming" in this book refers to the effects of this extra heat being trapped.

The Impact of Human Activities

Human activities generate three main greenhouse gases: **carbon dioxide**, **methane**, and **nitrous oxide**. Carbon dioxide is produced when **fossil fuels** such as coal and oil are burned. The level of carbon dioxide in the air is also affected by the clearing of forests, as trees and other plants absorb carbon dioxide to produce oxygen, which is vital to life on Earth. Methane is produced naturally by livestock such as cows and sheep who release it as part of their digestive process. It is also produced when substances such as manure and waste products in landfills begin to ferment, or turn sour. Nitrous oxide is produced when certain fertilizers are used to grow crops.

Fact ZONE
Without greenhouse gases the Earth's surface would have an average temperature of −0.4°F (−18°C).

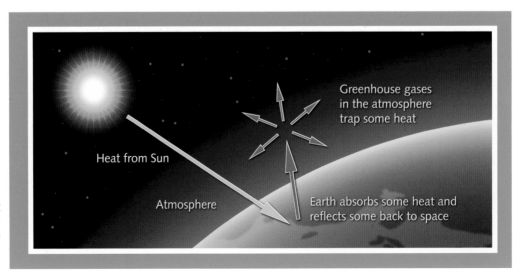

The greenhouse effect happens when certain gases in the atmosphere trap the Sun's heat.

Heat from Sun

Atmosphere

Greenhouse gases in the atmosphere trap some heat

Earth absorbs some heat and reflects some back to space

Possible Effects of Global Warming

Scientists are making predictions about the effects of global warming. Global warming could affect the environment and humans in many different ways.

POSSIBLE EFFECTS OF GLOBAL WARMING IN THE ANTARCTIC

POSSIBLE EVENT	PREDICTED RESULT	IMPACT IN THE ANTARCTIC
WARMER TEMPERATURES ON THE ANTARCTIC PENINSULA	✳ Break-up of the ice shelf ✳ Smaller area of winter sea ice ✳ Rising global sea levels	✳ Quicker movement of glaciers ✳ Danger of icebergs to ships in the area
SMALLER AREA OF WINTER SEA ICE	✳ Fewer **krill** and **phytoplankton**	✳ Decline in some species that rely on these food sources ✳ Reduced **habitat** and food supply for Adélie penguins
MORE SNOWFALL	✳ Faster moving ice sheet and glaciers	✳ More icebergs, which contribute to rising sea levels when they melt
REDUCED RECOVERY OF **OZONE LAYER**	✳ Fewer phytoplankton ✳ Less protection from damaging rays of the sun	✳ Decline in some species that rely on this food source ✳ Higher chance of eye and skin damage from the sun

Climate Change in the Antarctic

The Antarctic contains 90 percent of the world's ice and 70 percent of the world's freshwater. If this were all to melt, sea levels would rise by 197 to 213 feet (60 to 65 meters). This is probably the most alarming possible climate change event. The resulting flood would destroy most of the world's major coastal cities.

The Antarctic Peninsula

Temperatures on the Antarctic Peninsula have risen more quickly than the average global increase. This has caused some of the ice shelf to break up and melt. Some of this ice is frozen freshwater, so when it melts it will cause an increase in the sea level. The melting and freezing of seawater from year to year doesn't affect sea levels.

Ice shelves are an extension of glaciers over the sea. With the ice shelf of the Antarctic Peninsula melting, the glaciers have started **retreating** too, and at a faster rate. Glaciers that melt upon reaching the sea contribute to a small increase in sea levels.

Inland Antarctica

The average temperature of inland Antarctica is –35°F (–37°C) and it has remained stable for forty years. If temperatures rise a few degrees it will have no effect. Researchers agree that there will be some temperature increase over the next fifty years.

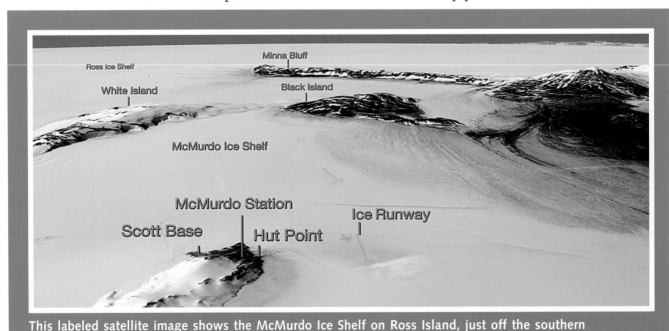

Ross Ice Shelf
Minna Bluff
White Island
Black Island
McMurdo Ice Shelf
McMurdo Station
Scott Base
Hut Point
Ice Runway

This labeled satellite image shows the McMurdo Ice Shelf on Ross Island, just off the southern coast of Antarctica.

Antarctic Food Chains

Warmer temperatures over the peninsula have already had an impact on wildlife. As the area of sea ice decreases, biologists have noted a dramatic reduction in krill, the major food source for many penguins. In the future there may be further impacts on the Antarctic **food chain**, in which krill play such a vital role.

More Snow

Warmer global temperatures are likely to cause increased snowfall over Antarctica. When this happens, the ice sheet and glaciers move faster. This will produce more icebergs, which will contribute to rising sea levels when they melt. Scientists are not sure whether increased snowfall will result in more ice developing over the continent in years to come.

Fact ZONE
An adult blue whale eats about four million krill each day.

Antarctic krill grow to about 2.4 inches (6 centimeters) long and are the main species of krill in the Antarctic.

The Natural World of the Antarctic

The Antarctic has spectacular natural features and large numbers of some wildlife species. Its remote location and harsh weather mean the area is largely untouched by humans.

Life in the Antarctic is only suited to a few tough types of plants and animals. Most of the wildlife lives on the sub-Antarctic islands, in the oceans, and the coastal areas of the continent, which are ice-free. Inland there are no signs of wildlife.

Ice Sheets and Ice Shelves

Ice is the dominant feature of Antarctica. It occurs as a vast ice sheet, covering the continent to an average depth of over 5,906 feet (1,800 m). Glaciers form on the ice sheet. This continental ice sheet extends out across the ocean where it is known as an ice shelf. As the ice shelf melts, huge chunks of ice, known as icebergs, separate from the shelf.

Fact ZONE

Antarctica is weighed down by its massive ice sheet. If it melted, the continent would "spring" back up by about 1,640 ft (500 m). This would take up to 10,000 years.

The Antarctic ice sheet is extremely thick.

Land-Based Ecosystems

Land-based **ecosystems**, which include **lichens** and mosses, occur mainly on the ice-free areas near the coast. The largest permanent land animal is an insect, a 0.4-inch (10-millimeter) midge. The continent is visited in summer by large numbers of seals, penguins, and other birds. The sub-Antarctic islands, spread across the Southern Ocean, are warmer and provide breeding grounds for huge colonies of seals, penguins, and sea birds.

Ocean Ecosystem

The Southern Ocean is full of life due to its high oxygen levels and plentiful food. It supports many unique fish species, which in turn support many sea birds. Shearwaters, terns, and petrels feed at sea and come ashore to breed. Eleven penguin species are found in the Antarctic, including Adélie and emperor penguins, which feed on krill, fish, and squid.

Whales have a thick layer of blubber to protect them from the cold. Baleen whales eat krill and small fish, which they filter through bristle-like plates in their mouths. Other resident whale species are the blue, southern right, and humpback whales, and toothed whales, such as the orca (killer whale).

Fact ZONE
Fish in the Southern Ocean have an antifreeze component in their blood so they don't freeze.

Penguins gather in large breeding colonies in the Antarctic.

11

Ice Shelves

Background

Antarctica is surrounded by ice shelves, which extend from the ice sheet over the surrounding ocean.

Ice shelves are floating blocks of ice fed by the continental ice sheet and glaciers. They also occur off the Antarctic Peninsula.

The Antarctic Peninsula is very sensitive to temperature change. The warmest parts of the Antarctic Peninsula have an average temperature of 23°F (–5°C). A small temperature increase can result in a few more days of melting each year. This warming is causing some ice shelves on the peninsula to start to break up.

These ice cliffs are part of the Ross Ice Shelf on the Antarctic Peninsula.

CASE STUDY

The Larsen B Ice Shelf

In January 2002 the Larsen B Ice Shelf broke up within 35 days, losing 1,255 square miles (3,250 square kilometers) of ice into the sea. This event shocked scientists because it happened so quickly to an ice sheet that had been developing for over 10,000 years. Warmer conditions resulted in melting pools of water on the shelf, which filled and deepened cracks in the ice. This weakened the ice shelf and it broke up into a series of icebergs up to 722 ft (220 m) high. The melting of floating ice such as the Larsen B Ice Shelf will cause some increase in sea levels. It will also cause the glaciers that flow onto the ice shelf to move faster. Their meltwater would add to global sea levels.

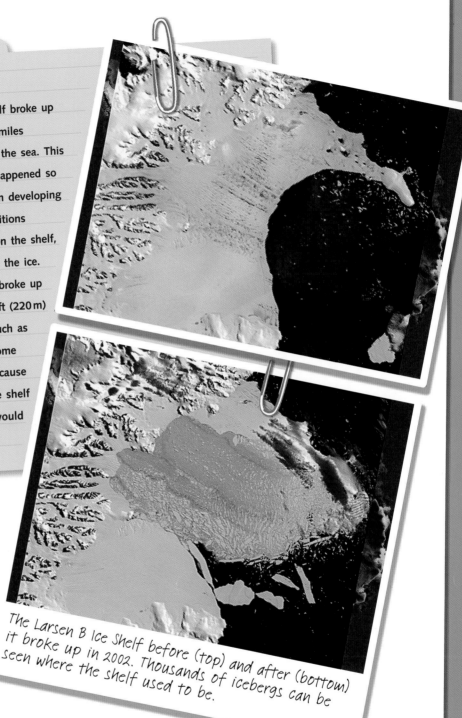

The Larsen B Ice Shelf before (top) and after (bottom) it broke up in 2002. Thousands of icebergs can be seen where the shelf used to be.

Glaciers

Background

The Antarctic ice sheet covering the continent is made from snow that has fallen and been compressed into ice over thousands of years.

Under the ice are mountains and valleys. Where mountains occur the ice flows into valleys to form rivers of ice called glaciers. These move slowly toward the coast, pushed by the ice behind them and pulled by gravity.

When a glacier reaches the coast it may flow onto an ice shelf or break off into the open water to produce icebergs. Global warming is causing glaciers on the peninsula to move faster, and their meltwater may eventually cause sea levels to rise.

Fact ZONE

Snow falling at the South Pole takes 100,000 years to "flow" to the Antarctic coast and drop off as part of an iceberg.

Calving is the name used to describe the formation of icebergs from glaciers or ice sheets.

Retreating Peninsula Glaciers

On the Antarctic Peninsula global warming has caused 84 percent of all glaciers to retreat by about 1,969 ft (600 m). In the past fifty years temperatures have risen by 4.5°F (2.5°C) on the Antarctic Peninsula. Since the breakup of the Larsen B Ice Shelf, glaciers flow eight times faster.

Higher temperatures are causing some of the glacier ice to melt. The meltwater helps glaciers to flow faster. Glaciers are said to be retreating when the amount of melting at the end of the glacier is greater than the movement of the glacier down a valley. There is not enough ice replacing the ice that has melted.

Although the meltwater from these glaciers is not enough to significantly affect sea levels, these levels could rise if climate change affects areas further south, where glaciers are much larger.

The Lambert Fisher Glacier in Antarctica, the largest on Earth, is 249 miles (400 kilometers) long, 25 miles (40 km) wide, and up to 8,202 ft (2,500 m) thick.

Adélie Penguins

Background

Adélie penguins are the smallest of the Antarctic penguin species. They are around 30 inches (75 centimeters) in height and weigh about 11 pounds (5 kilograms).

These otherwise flightless birds are able to "fly" through the water using their wings. Their overlapping feathers trap air, which insulates them from the cold.

They live in huge colonies, which protect them from predators such as leopard seals, sea lions, and orca (killer whales).

Due to global warming, Adélie penguin numbers are dropping. Global warming is affecting the penguins' food supply and its habitat.

Fact ZONE
There are 193 breeding colonies and around 2.5 million breeding pairs of Adélie penguins in the Antarctic.

Adélie penguins are great swimmers, able to dive up to 574 ft (175 m) in search of food.

Reduced Food Supply

The Adélie penguin's main food source is krill. Krill numbers have dropped dramatically in the waters off the Antarctic Peninsula. The phytoplankton that krill feed on are in short supply because global warming has reduced the area of winter sea ice, under which they grow. As a result, there are fewer krill and the Adélie penguin has less food to eat.

Reduced Habitat

Adélie penguin numbers on the Antarctic Peninsula have declined by up to 65 percent in the past twenty-five years. Adélie penguins live on the sea ice for much of the year and use it as a base for feeding. As their habitat has been reduced so have their numbers. Scientists fear the penguins may abandon their breeding colonies there completely.

Competition for Territory

Researchers have found that as Adélie penguin numbers drop chinstrap penguin have invaded their territory. The chinstrap penguin eats a wider variety of food and prefers open water so it is better suited to the changes in climate.

Adélie penguins (front left) have to compete with chinstrap penguins (front right) for territory.

The impact of climate change on...

The Ozone Layer

Background

Ozone is a gas in Earth's atmosphere. The ozone layer absorbs harmful **ultraviolet light** from the sun. When the ozone layer is damaged this light reaches Earth and can cause skin cancer, eye cataracts, and damage to crops.

The Earth's ozone layer has been damaged by chemicals called **chlorofluorocarbons (CFCs)**. Until recently, these chemicals were widely used in spray cans, refrigerators, and air conditioners.

CFCs remain in the atmosphere for more than one hundred years, so although we have largely stopped using them they are still causing damage to the ozone layer.

Every spring the ozone layer becomes thinner over Antarctica. CFCs are activated by Antarctic winter temperatures, then the spring sunlight sets off a reaction that destroys the ozone, forming a hole. Scientists have linked global warming and ozone destruction in a number of ways.

Fact ZONE
In 2003 the hole in the ozone layer was three times larger than the United States.

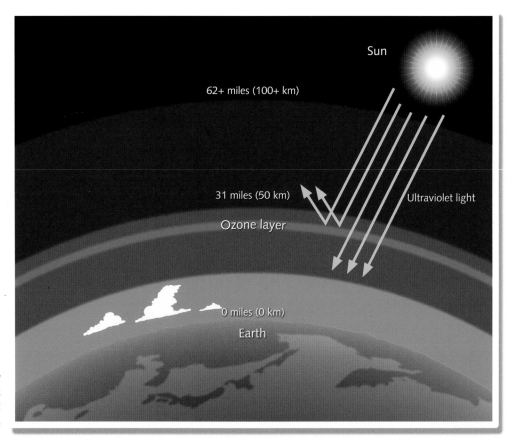

The ozone layer protects us from some ultraviolet light.

Slower Ozone Recovery

Scientists think that global warming may reduce the recovery of the hole in the ozone layer. Global warming traps heat in the lower parts of the atmosphere. The upper atmosphere, where the ozone layer is found, then becomes colder, which damages the ozone layer.

The ozone hole may be partly responsible for reduced numbers of the ocean's phytoplankton, a vital part of ocean food chains. Increased ultraviolet light reaching the ocean surface causes the phytoplankton to sink deeper into the water, which reduces their growth and breeding rate.

Double Destruction

Research has found that CFCs, which destroy the ozone layer, are responsible for about 10 percent of global warming. These gases are destroying the ozone layer and contributing to global warming by slowing its recovery.

Fact ZONE

Phytoplankton absorb some of the Sun's rays, which would normally be reflected back to space. Fewer phytoplankton as a result of ozone damage, would lower the phytoplankton's contribution to global warming.

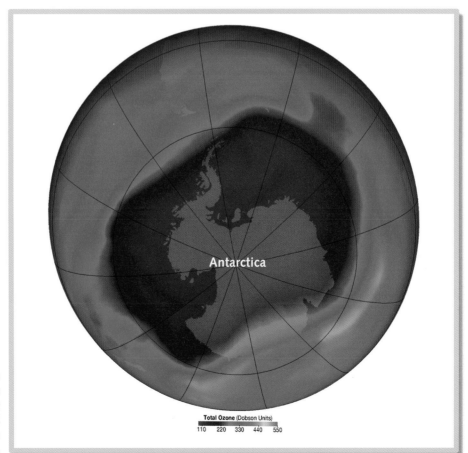

Total Ozone (Dobson Units)
110   220   330   440   550

Antarctica

This image shows the ozone layer above Antarctica in the spring of 2006. The blue and purple regions indicate low levels of ozone.

The impact of climate change on...

Krill and Antarctic Food Chains

Background

Krill are small shrimplike animals found by the billion in the cold waters of the Antarctic. They grow up to 2.4 inches (6 cm) in length, weigh less than an ounce, and can live up to ten years.

They are usually found in deep water but swim to the surface up to three times a day to feed on algae. They return to deeper water after feeding to avoid being eaten by predators.

Fact ZONE

In 1981 a swarm of krill tracked by scientists was estimated to weigh 9.8 million tons (10 million tonnes). This is equivalent to 143 million people weighing an average of 154 pounds (70 kilograms) each.

Krill forms a vital part of the Antarctic food chain. A food chain shows the feeding links between plants and animals in an ecosystem. Global warming is affecting krill numbers, which could have a dramatic effect on the food chain.

Krill are extremely important to the Antarctic food chain.

Disappearing Krill and the Antarctic Food Chain

Today, the number of Antarctic krill is only one-fifth of the number thirty years ago. The diagram below shows the impact on the Antarctic food chain.

Sea ice, which is frozen seawater, plays an important role in the Antarctic food chain. It is a source of food for krill, who feed on the algae that grow on the underside of the sea ice. Krill, in turn, are eaten by fish. Fewer algae and krill would lower the number of fish and this would impact whales and penguins, which feed on the fish. Some penguin populations on Antarctic islands have already declined by up to 50 percent.

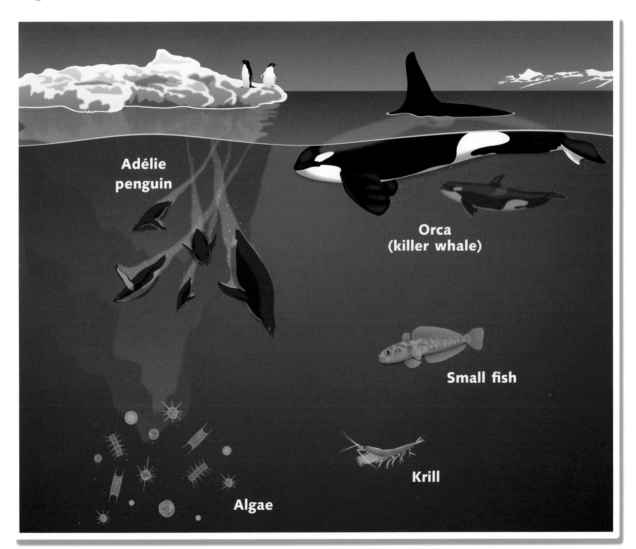

A change in one part of this Antarctic food chain affects every other part of the chain.

Humans in the Antarctic

The Antarctic's harsh climate has protected it from development and settlement by nearby countries. It has no permanent population and there are no cities or towns. The only people who "live" in the Antarctic usually stay for one or two years to conduct research.

Territorial Claims

No nation owns Antarctica but seven countries claimed territory before 1959. Australia claimed 42 percent of the continent. Norway, Argentina, New Zealand, France, Great Britain, and Chile have all staked claims to part of the continent. Some of these territorial claims overlap, creating the possibility of tension. In 1959 the Antarctic Treaty was signed by countries interested in the region. The signing of the treaty meant that Antarctica was set aside for peaceful purposes and for free scientific investigation. Countries agreed to set aside all future territorial claims, and all military activity is banned.

Fact ZONE
In 2006 over 29,000 people visited the Antarctic.

Tourism

Tourism in Antarctica is increasing. Visitors come to see the stunning scenery and the wildlife. There are no land-based tourist facilities such as hotels, so visitors stay on ships.

Antarctica is becoming a more popular tourist destination.

Scientific Bases

Today there are seventy-four scientific research bases on Antarctica. Most of the bases are located in the few ice-free areas, usually along the coast and on the Antarctic Peninsula. During summer about four thousand scientists come to study natural features such as rocks, ice, weather, and wildlife.

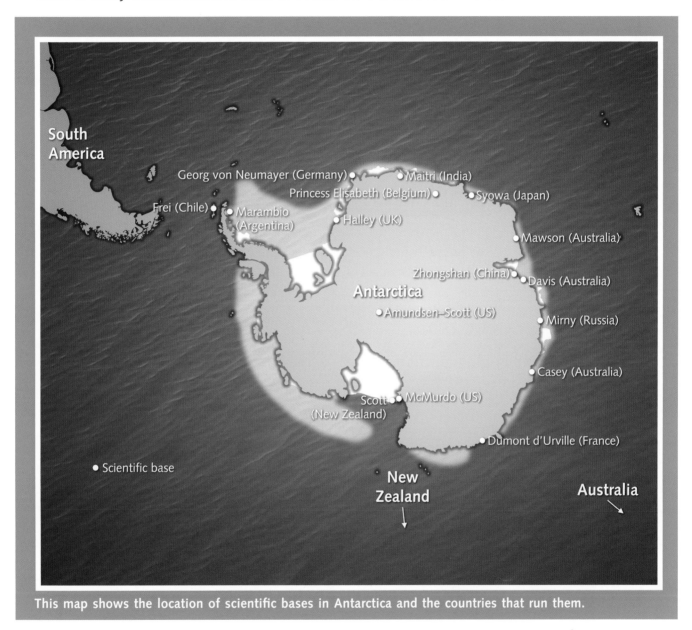

This map shows the location of scientific bases in Antarctica and the countries that run them.

Antarctic Research

Background

The Antarctic is a popular place for research on climate change. Air bubbles in the Antarctic ice sheet contain evidence of past climate change. The Antarctic air is some of the cleanest on Earth, making it ideal for scientists to study changes to the atmosphere.

Scientific Research

The Antarctic ice sheet contains a record of past climate change. **Ice cores** taken by scientists called glaciologists contain air trapped as bubbles. Scientists analyze this air to learn what the atmosphere was like in the past.

Air bubbles in ice cores contain valuable information about the atmosphere of the past.

Analyzing Ice

Ice cores taken from below the surface of Antarctica at depths of up to 1.9 miles (3 km) show that current levels of the greenhouse gases carbon dioxide and methane are higher now than at any time in the past 650,000 years.

Climate change scientists are also studying the ice sheet, valley glaciers, and ice shelves, observing any changes in thickness, size, and speed of movement.

Studying Phytoplankton

Researchers are also investigating climate change in the Southern Ocean. Oceans absorb about one-third of all carbon dioxide. Much of this is absorbed by phytoplankton. Warmer seas prevent the upward movement of phytoplankton's food. This is causing these plants to die, which could release more greenhouse gas into the atmosphere. Carbon dioxide dissolves more easily into cold water so the Southern Ocean has been the center of this research.

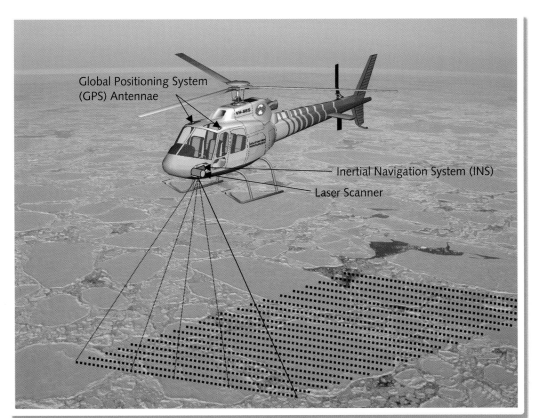

Global Positioning System (GPS) Antennae

Inertial Navigation System (INS)

Laser Scanner

The latest technology is being used to measure changes to the ice shelf and glaciers. GPS and INS enable accurate navigation while the laser scanner determines how thick a specified area of ice is (shown here as black dots).

Carbon Footprints

Background

Carbon footprints are a measure of the carbon dioxide humans produce while doing their activities. This footprint is a very powerful tool in understanding the contribution each person makes to global warming.

Working in a relatively untouched and fragile environment, researchers have a special awareness of the need to reduce their carbon footprint while in the Antarctic. Although the carbon footprint in the Antarctic is relatively small, the action of scientists to reduce it sets a good example.

Fact ZONE

Each of the following activities adds 2.2 lb (1 kg) of carbon dioxide to the atmosphere:

- driving a car 4 miles (6 km)
- operating a computer for thirty-two hours
- manufacturing five plastic bags

All of these activities contribute to your carbon footprint.

New Zealand Response: Wind Farm

New Zealand is planning to build a wind farm at its Antarctic base. The wind turbines will be linked to the electric grids of McMurdo Station (United States) and Scott Base (New Zealand). The project will reduce fossil fuel use by 11 percent and reduce carbon emissions by 1,222 tons (1,242 tonnes) a year.

Wind turbines at Scott Base will be similar to those at Australia's Mawson Base, shown here.

Community Response: Carbon Footprint

In 2007 the International Association of Antarctic Tour Operators discussed the impact of tourism on the Antarctic. Over sixty-six tour operators agreed to measure their carbon footprint and develop ways to reduce their carbon emissions. Tourism is already controlled by a code of conduct to minimize pollution and disturbances to wildlife.

Tour operators have agreed to reduce the carbon footprint of tourism in the Antarctic.

The Future

The Antarctic is a unique wilderness where scientists from around the world visit and study in a spirit of cooperation. Antarctic ice is a valuable source of information about climate change and global warming.

The Antarctic Peninsula

Ice cores taken from the Antarctic show that levels of greenhouse gases are increasing. The rapid breakup of ice sheets and the increased flow of glaciers on the Antarctic Peninsula have concerned scientists. These events look dramatic but will add little to global sea levels. Fortunately the extreme cold in most of Antarctica will prevent the continental ice sheet from melting.

Food Chains

Global warming could change the Antarctic food chain in the future. If the amounts of phytoplankton and krill are reduced, animals and birds higher in the food chain, such as the Adélie penguin, will have less to eat and their numbers may fall.

Sharing Science

Antarctica's ice contains the secrets of Earth's past climate. The results of the shared work of international scientists in the Antarctic may be very important in the future.

Fact ZONE

Many people would like to see Antarctica listed as a **World Heritage Area,** so it would continue to be a global model of peace and cooperation.

Scientific cooperation is important in climate change research in Antarctica.

Glossary

atmosphere	the layer of gases that surrounds Earth
carbon dioxide	a greenhouse gas produced by burning fossil fuels and clearing forests
carbon footprint	a measure of the carbon dioxide humans produce while doing their activities
chlorofluorocarbons	chemicals that damage the ozone layer
climate change	changes in weather patterns caused by global warming
ecosystem	a group of living things and their habitat
extinction	the death of every member of a group of living things
food chain	an ordered linkage of living things. Living things higher in the order eat the living things below them in the chain
fossil fuel	a fuel such as coal or oil made of fossilized remains of plants
glaciers	slow-moving frozen rivers of ice
global warming	an increase in the average surface temperature of Earth
greenhouse effect	the warming of Earth's surface due to trapping of heat by the atmosphere
greenhouse gas	a gas that helps trap the sun's heat in the atmosphere
habitat	the surroundings in which an animal or plant lives
Ice Age	a period when temperatures were lower and large areas of Earth were ice-covered
iceberg	a floating piece of ice that has broken off an ice shelf
ice core	a sample of ice taken from within an ice sheet
ice sheet	a thick layer of ice covering Antarctica
ice shelf	layers of floating ice still attached to the mainland
krill	small shrimplike animals
Kyoto Protocol	a special guideline that was created with the aim of reducing greenhouse gases
lichen	a small flat plant made of a fungus and algae growing together
methane	a greenhouse gas produced by cattle and rotting plant material
nitrous oxide	a greenhouse gas produced from fertilizers
ozone layer	the protective layer in the upper atmosphere
phytoplankton	a microscopic plant that forms the basis of the Antarctic food chain
renewable energy	energy from virtually unlimited sources, such as the sun
retreating	moving backward
sea ice	ice that forms from the freezing of sea water
ultraviolet light	a type of invisible radiation from the sun
United Nations	a group of countries that have agreed to work together on matters such as peace, security, and cooperation
World Heritage Area	a special area of outstanding beauty or cultural importance that is protected for the benefit of future generations

Index